'Nobby' Clarke
Churchill's 'backroom boy'

Bernard O'Connor

Every reasonable effort has been made to locate, contact and acknowledge copyright holders of quotes and illustrations used in my work. They have been credited within the text and/or in the bibliography. Much appreciation is given to those who have agreed that I include their work. Any copyright owners who are not properly identified and acknowledged, get in touch so that I may make any necessary corrections.

Bernard O'Connor

Visit my website at
http://www.bernardoconnor.org.uk

'Nobby' Clarke

Churchill's 'backroom boy'

Introduction

Having moved in 1992 to the village of Everton in northeast Bedfordshire, I started researching the history of the nearby RAF Tempsford, a remote airfield about fifty miles north of London. It was used as a base for 138 and 161 Squadrons during World War Two, from where they flew on top secret missions to supply the various resistance groups in occupied Europe. I have published a number of books on the subject and was investigating the buildings requisitioned by the Special Operations Executive (SOE), a clandestine organisation set up in 1940 with a request from Winston Churchill "to set Europe ablaze', and its American equivalent, the Office of Strategic Services (OSS). Most were used to accommodate and train secret agents who afterwards were taken to RAF Tempsford to be either parachuted by the Royal Air Forces' Special Duties Squadrons from a Halifax or Stirling aircraft or landed by a Lysander or Hudson. As well as helping organize resistance activities, some were sent as radio operators and some specialized in explosives and sabotage.

In a list detailing the locations used by the OSS I noticed 'Area K Bedford, Special Operations - Demolition School'. Intrigued, I tried to locate where exactly in Bedford it was, who was involved and what role it played during the war. I contacted The Bedfordshire and Luton Archive Service and Lydia Saul, Keeper of Social History, at the Cecil Higgins Gallery Bedford Museum. In particular I'd like to acknowledge the reminiscences of John Clarke, an Old Boy from Bedford School and Ann Hagen at Bedford Museum who transcribed them for the BBC's WW2 People's War website. They revealed that his father, Cecil Vandepeer Clarke, had a property on Tavistock Street in Bedford that the Americans called 'Area K'. On contacting John's wife, Anne, she very kindly supplied me with photographs and other documents about her father-in-law's secret war work and gave me permission to include them in this work. I also need to thank the staff at the National Archives and acknowledge Stephen Bunker's *Spy Capital of Britain* and Stuart Macrae's *Winston Churchill's Toyshop* .

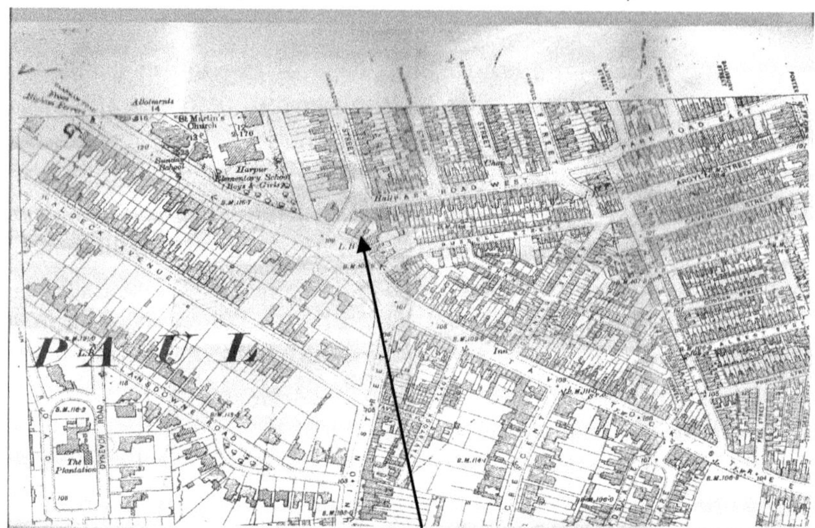

Extract from 1901 25" OS Map of Bedford showing Nobby Clarke's workshops behind 171-175 Tavistock Street.

Major Cecil 'Nobby' Vandepeer Clarke - designer and producer of top secret weaponry during World War Two. (Courtesy of Ann Clarke)

Born on 15th February 1897, Cecil Vandepeer Clarke grew up in London and was known to his friends as Nobby. He attended Greenwich Hospital School and the Grocers' Company School but when the First World War broke out in 1914, he abandoned his studies at the University of London for a two year certificate course with the Officer Training Corps. After getting an 'A' in the Combined Training Course, in 1915 he was gazetted as a 2nd Lieutenant in the Devonshire Regiment. Transferred to the 9th Battalion South Staffordshire Regiment, 23rd Division, he served as a Captain in the British Expeditionary Force in France. In October 1917 he was sent to Italy where he was awarded the Military Cross for taking part in the decisive battle of Vittorio Veneto. During that time he served as an Officer in a Pioneer Battalion which involved doing a great deal of tunnelling and general explosives work. In fact, he was said to have loved making loud bangs.

After the Armistice was signed in 1919, he moved to Bedford and became director of the motor manufacturing firm, H.P. Webb and Co. Ltd. In 1924 he bought 172-3 Tavistock Street, a residential property with an adjacent commercial garage and started his own motor engineering firm. (TNA HS 9/321.8)

In his spare time he built his own four cylinder motor car engine in the workshop behind the premises. However, his new product did not make money as the major car manufacturers of the time could produce similar engines more cheaply. He realised that there was a space in the market for trailers of one kind or another. Most two-wheeled trailers were unstable when pulled behind a vehicle, so he designed them with a low-slung chassis, close coupled wheels and a special suspension system. Accordingly, he set up his own business, LoLode (Low Loading Trailer Company), which specialised in manufacturing low loading trailers that could be towed behind vehicles.

'Nobby' married Dorothy Aileen in August 1928 and they had three children, John, David and Roger. His eldest son, John Clarke, dictated his reminiscences of his childhood in pre-war

Bedford to Ann Hagen of Bedford Museum. These form the basis of much of this booklet. Whilst some are long, they are worth including as they are a first-hand account of wartime Bedford, life at school and the top secret work his father was involved with.

As a child John attended Froebel Teaching College School in The Crescent under the guidance of a Miss Spence.

We used to trot along the 200 or 300 yards to the very friendly atmosphere of the school. I stayed there until I was nine or ten when I passed the entrance exam to go to Bedford School in the Preparatory Department.

Before the war Bedford was a much smaller town, it was only about 40,000 population and we had a very quiet life. There was a regular pattern of school, and holidays were generally spent in the town but every summer we would have a fortnight's holiday away, generally in South Wales. My father and mother would take us off to The Gower for a wonderful time on the beach and on the cliffs there in South Wales.

When I'd finished at the Training College School and went to Bedford School, this was in 1938 at the time of the Munich Crisis. By which time my father was getting very concerned as an ex-Army Officer from the First World War when he had won the M.C. (Military Cross) for his work in Italy and France; he was getting very concerned that the country was heading for another war with Germany. He started making preparations for what might happen and I remember trenches being dug and Air Raid Precautions starting and I believe he was the ARP [Air Raid Precaution] *Officer for Bedford, for the period immediately before the war.*

I used to go again on foot up Tavistock Street. It must be the most familiar street to me from my memories of Bedford, full of shops some of which haven't changed at all since that time. Up to the corner of De Parys Avenue and

THE EARLY GARAGES 81

A front view of J. Crawley & Sons in Tavistock Street, with no. 171 (right), 1950s. In this house which was part of the premises, Captain Cecil Vandepeer Clarke worked on the prototype of the limpet-mine at the beginning of the Second World War. (AC)

J. Crawley & Sons bought the former Low Loading Trailer Company premises at 171–5 Tavistock Street in the late 1940s. This side view taken in the 1950s shows the corner with Clarendon Street (left) and the outbuildings used by Captain Clarke. (AC)

(Wildman, R. and Crawley, (2003), A. *Bedford's Motor Heritage, Sutton Publishing*) *initially to the Preparatory Department, the Prep School known as the Inky at Bedford School where I was for two years. I was in the top class and I did fairly well. We were taught in the first year by a very pleasant young exchange teacher from Canada whose name was Mr. P. A. Bridle and he was known actually to us children as 'Pa'. He got us in the first year into the rudiments of school life at Bedford School and left after a year. He was in fact lucky to survive his return journey which had started before the war. But as he was on the liner Athenia, he had the unlucky distinction of being one of the first people to be sunk by a German U boat only a day or two after the commencement of war in 1939. [On 3 September 1939, over 100 lost their lives.]*

I remember September the 3rd, 1939 very clearly standing to attention in our house while the National Anthem was played and hearing [Neville] *Chamberlain* [the then Prime Minister] *speaking. We had help in the house because my mother was the Company Secretary of the Low Loading Trailer Company; therefore we had a maid and we had a cook as well. We could hear they were in tears in the kitchen as they heard the news. Then a few minutes later the air raid sirens sounded but it was a false alarm. It sounded over London and I think for good measure they thought they'd better include Bedford, just in case German planes came over.*

(http://www.bbc.co.uk/ww2peopleswar/stories/34/a5961134.shtml)

By 1937 Nobby had designed the chassis for a 'double-decker' caravan and had a local Bedford company make the coachworks. It had a built-in toilet and separate shower with hot and cold running water. He claimed that passengers could sit in the main saloon and pour out drinks without spilling them.

Despite of the economic and political problems during the late 1930s 'Nobby' ensured that his family had a chance to get away from it all. John recalled how

We went on holiday with our lovely caravan which by that time, because myself and my younger brother, three years younger than me, were getting larger and larger. My father decided to take the unusual step of having the original 1937 caravan with its wonderful lines somewhat spoiled. It was but not too bad looking but very unusual looking, providing a second storey on the caravan. So we had a double-decker caravan with room for the boys, that's myself and my brother, to sleep in the upstairs accommodation which we reached by a ladder coming down off the back of the caravan, out of doors. I distinctly remember in 1939 we went on holiday after all the experimentation on the limpet mine had been completed; we went to North Wales and we had to be very careful because there were a great number of low bridges. Every time, as we left Bedford, we would stop if there was a low railway bridge and approach very cautiously to see whether we'd got the inch or two clearance we needed to get through without taking the caravan top off. But after a while I must say my father, temperamentally he got rather blasé about this and just charged at every bridge he came to - fortunately without any real damage to the caravan. I remember going through North Wales, standing, which I'm sure would be contrary to Health and Safety Regulations today, on the catwalk on the roof of the original caravan outside of our cabin and getting a fine view of the countryside as we went along the A5 through North Wales. Then we came back and the war started.

(http://www.bbc.co.uk/ww2peopleswar/stories/34/a5961134.shtml)

Life at Bedford School during World War Two was very different for John. In his reminiscences he recalled how

"... we had a much more Spartan regime I think than before the war. But it was only gradually introduced

because, for example, important things like the Tuck Shop where you could buy sweets and chocolate at the School was well stocked up in the first few months at the beginning of the war. So it was only gradually that the pain of deprivation from familiar things like bananas and oranges and so on really hit home. But quite apart from that, life was extremely disciplined at Bedford School in those days. We were a public school with a long tradition, founded in 1552, and everybody was very carefully monitored and looked after but it was a very busy school regime. We would start as usual as most schools at about 9 o'clock in the morning. I was a 'day boy' and I should say that 30-40% of the boys at the school were in boarding houses grouped around the School Campus. I was one of the 'day boys' at the school and my brothers subsequently went to Bedford School. The typical school day would be arriving at school just before 9 o'clock, two hours in the morning period, then break for 20 minutes. This was not an uncontrolled sort of break but was very disciplined in that we were marched out by Forms and were taken by senior boys who were either Monitors or Options, in other words, Prefects, either senior or junior in status, to do physical exercises. PE, very vigorously for about a quarter of an hour which left us about five minutes to chat with friends and then back to work for the second half of the morning session. Then we had prayers and having had Morning Assembly first of all we would have brief prayers at 1 o'clock and then go home. If we were living close enough, we could go home for our lunch and be back within the hour. In the afternoons we had on Mondays, Wednesdays and Fridays we had further school lessons until about 4 o'clock.

But on Tuesdays, Thursdays and Saturdays, these were Games days. And the usual sort of regime with rugger in the winter months, rowing in the winter months and in the summer too and cricket in the summer with a whole host of minor sports which everyone was supposed to enjoy and many people did. I particularly enjoyed playing 'Fives' but apart from that there were things like gymnastics, boxing and so on as extra curriculum things. You were expected to do your ordinary games and then in addition to that you were normally expected to take part in some secondary sport. So sport was a very important part of the Bedford School experience.

We also, as I got further up the school, we found ourselves in the JTC, that's the Junior Training Corp which was originally, in the First World War, had been called the Officer Training Corps and then it was the Junior Training Corps and later on I believe it was given another name CCF - (Combined Cadet Force). We were in the JTC and then I found an opportunity to escape from the JTC which meant that we had in the JTC Regular Army training under the auspices of Sergeant Majors who were on the school staff. I found that I was able, during the latter part of the war, to transfer to the ATC, the Air Training Corps which was slightly less military and more interesting because we had the occasional opportunity of having a flight in the Royal Air Force planes at nearby aerodromes either at Henlow or Cranfield. I enjoyed a couple of very nice trips in Avro bi-planes. As one of the perks of belonging to the ATC we were supposed to know all about aeroplanes and identification and so on; I don't think any of us got terribly good at it but it was preferable to being in khaki. One thing I was very pleased that I did not have to do in the ATC was to participate in the wrong part of a group which went out to Cranfield. We were split up for flight experience. We were split into two groups, this was probably 1945, and half of us went up in a perfectly innocuous bi-plane and I was allocated as part of that group. I was very pleased I was on that side because the others were invited to, or told, to take their places in a glider and we watched the glider being towed up. That was alright but when it came down we were astonished to see the glider, detached of course from the towing aircraft, coming down at an angle of about 45° degrees at great speed until it was about 20 feet above the ground, it suddenly flattened out and it landed. I'm afraid that my friends who had drawn the wrong ticket came out looking extremely green! Laughter! As a result I was very pleased that I had not had to participate in glider training. I think this was a normal landing technique. They gathered enough speed to come down at the right angle. Anyway we watched horror stricken as this thing came down. We thought all our friends had had it. A view that was much more intensely felt by those on the glider!

Our holidays in the war years were necessarily not the same sort of pattern as before the war. We had to spend time in Bedfordshire primarily. We had School Camps as I got into the upper part of the school and we had a very enjoyable time harvesting one summer (about 1942 or 1943) in Stewartby at the Brick Works. In their model village at Stewartby they had a few spare empty houses and we were accommodated there and well fed in the London Brick Works canteen. These were all very new buildings at that time because the estate was only built in the 1930s. We were taken out on trucks to help bring in the harvest, stooking and so on in the nearby farms which were in fact in the ownership of the Brick Company which had valuable resources of clay for brick making underneath them. At that time the London Brick Company had no need or intention to obtain. They had acquired a whole series of farms in this clay bearing area so that for future development they could get their clay for making bricks. I well remember our lunches were uniformly bread and dripping [beef fat] *throughout the three weeks I think of our time in harvesting.*

(http://www.bbc.co.uk/ww2peopleswar/stories/52/a5961152.shtml)

When Nobby submitted an advertisement for inclusion in the journal *Caravan & Trailer*, it brought him to the attention of its editor, Stuart Macrae, who also edited the *'Science Armchair'* magazine. Macrae visited Nobby's workshop to inspect the caravan and, in *Winston Churchill's Toyshop,* his memoirs about his war years, described him as

> '... *a very large man with rather hesitant speech, who at first struck me as being amiable but not outstandingly bright. The second part of the impression did not last long.*'
>
> (Macrae, S. (1971), *Winston Churchill's Toyshop*p.p.8)

He subsequently wrote what was described as a very favourable article about the caravan which must have generated some trade and forged a link between the two men. In June 1939 Macrea was entrusted by the War Office's M.I.R.c. (Military Intelligence Research) section with the task of producing a magnetic device that could be attached to the hull of a ship and explode after a time delay, Impressed at the way 'Nobby' dealt with problems in an unorthodox way, he decided that he might be able to help.

> *Although I had not seen him since this initial visit, Clarke's unusual personality and his ability to view mechanical problems in an unorthodox way had always stuck in my mind. I decided that he was the man for me, jumped into my motorcar complete with rough drawings and my collection of magnets, and went off to Bedford. I had of course rung up Clarke to warn him that I was coming and given him a very guarded idea of what I wanted to talk about. He was operating from his private house which he had converted in some remarkable way into a works. Sweeping a number of children out of his living room which had also to serve as an office, he filled me with bread and jam and some awful buns and then we got down to business. Nobby, as I soon came to call him, was enthusiastic as I knew he would be. 'Fine! How about starting tomorrow? Be here as early as you can. Stay here if you like; we can easily find you a bed.'*
>
> (Macrae, S. (1971), *Winston Churchill's Toyshop*p.p.8)

This link extended throughout the Second World War and involved top secret work for Winston Churchill and the Special Operations Executive. The scientists and technicians who were involved in the design and manufacture of top secret weaponry were called 'boffins' or 'backroom boys'.

To assist him in his project, Nobby used the outbuildings behind the family home as an experimental workshop. John recalled his father often being in the workshop during the first months of the war, working on a limpet mine, a top secret new weapon with enormous potential for the war effort.

When, in 1939, Macrae was asked by somebody in the War Office if he could assist with the procurement or getting information where such things could be procured, whether he could supply or find a supplier for limpets and he was not told initially what they were for. But after his security clearance had been established with the War Office, Macrae was told that the idea was to provide limpet mines that could sink enemy shipping. So he said, 'I will do my best to design something with a colleague of mine whom I know and the two of us together, I think we can produce something for the use of British Forces.'

He'd got a short time but as he said, he'd got 'a bag of gold' from the War Office to do everything that was necessary. He contacted my father and came down to Bedford and the two got on very well - they'd known each other before because of the caravan experience. They cleared all the children out of the room where they were discussing the matter and then started to get the design together. It was very much an ad hoc way of approaching the thing but both were brilliant at lateral thinking and the two men within about a month (this was in June/July 1939) before the war, had evolved a practicable Mark I type of limpet mine.

As the eldest boy, I was then 10 years old, I took a keen

interest in what was going on and I knew broadly speaking what this was about. I was told not to say anything about it to my schoolboy friends. But the interesting thing about the limpet mine was that it was very much Bedford home made. The two men visited Woolworths and they got washing up bowls made of spun aluminium to contain the explosives.

(http://www.bbc.co.uk/ww2peopleswar/stories/34/a5961134.shtml)

Macrae recalled them cajoling a local tinsmith into stopping all the other work he was doing and fashion some rims with annular grooves to fit the bowls and plates they had bought. These were then screwed in place to allow the rims to close.

The rims were sweated to the bowls and as many of the little horseshoe magnets as possible were packed into the annular grooves so that the pole pieces were exposed, these pole pieces then being lined up by simply placing a keeper ring over the whole lot. To secure the magnets in place we at first poured bitumen into the groove, but later found that plaster of Paris was a better answer.

The idea was to stuff this bowl full of blasting gelatin or some similar high explosive and then screw the lid in place so that the device was sealed. It had to be carried by a swimmer, so we contrived a belt consisting of a 4" wide steel plate, just long enough to span the magnet ring, to which were attached strips of webbing which could be tied round the swimmer's waist. Obviously the swimmer must not be unduly handicapped by having to travel under water with this contrivance so we wanted it to weigh next to nothing when submerged. Eventually, after using up all the porridge in the house in place of high explosive for filling, juggling about with weights and dimensions, and flooding Nobby's bathroom on several occasions, we got this right.

(http://www.bbc.co.uk/ww2peopleswar/stories/34/a5961134.shtml)

After testing it in his bath, the field trials took place in

Photograph of Major Clarke showing original limpet with square pack of magnets and Woolworth's washbowl cover. This model is fitted with the aniseed 1-hour time delay. 24 of these were constructed filled with 5 lbs of blasting gelatine and flown out from Poole to Costanza for operational use against German oil tanker barges plying on the Danube within a few days of the outbreak of the war.
(Courtesy of Ann Clarke)

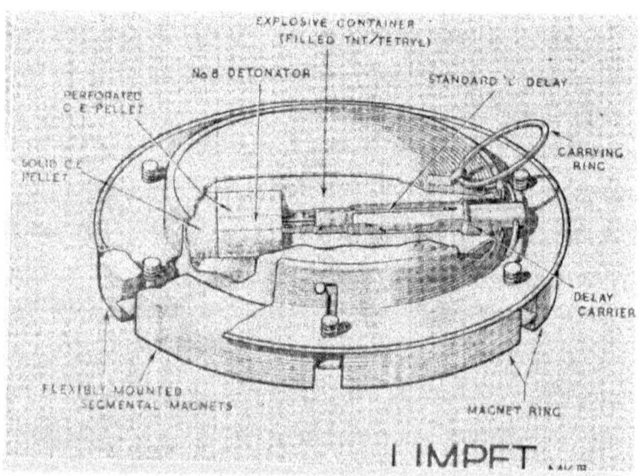

Diagram of the Limpet mine in Macrae's *Churchill's Toy Shop'*

Limpets and harness used by saboteurs to blow up transformers in France and 'Limpeteers' to sink enemy shipping.
(Courtesy of Ann Clarke)

Bedford Baths, which belonged to Bedford Modern School at the top of Clarendon Street, only about 200 yards away from the Clarke's household. Given the nature of their experiments, the baths were closed to the public during these tests. A large steel plate was propped up against the wall of the deep end to represent the side of a ship. Macrae appreciated Nobby being an excellent swimmer.

> *Looking as if he were suffering from advanced pregnancy he would swim to and fro removing the device from his belt, turning it over, and plonking it on the target plate with great skill. We learned a lot more than when we had been in the bathroom. Our magnets were so powerful that when in the water it at first proved difficult to remove the mine from the keeper plate belt without the risk of rupturing oneself. So we had to experiment with various sizes of plate until we had one which gave the required hold and no more. The buoyancy too came in for adjustment as we found it advantageous to have slight positive buoyancy.*
>
> (Macrae, op.cit.p.9)

John was often taken along to watch, and presumably enjoy swimming in an otherwise empty pool. He recalled that,

> *A swimmer would be loaded up with the limpet mines before swimming to the side of a ship and plant the charge against the side using magnets on the underside of the limpet mine. Hence the curved shape with the magnets underneath it looked like a gigantic limpet when it was attached to the hull of a ship. My father gallantly undertook all these tests himself with a steel plate strapped around his tummy and the charge on the limpet mine attached to it. He had quite a lot of problems with adjusting the number of magnets to be used. If it was too strong you just couldn't*

get the thing off and were struggling underwater with a very heavy metal casing on your tummy.

... There they were, swimming up and down and plonking them on a steel plate at the deep end and this worked well. Then to simulate the effect of a ship having had a limpet mine planted on it, all unsuspected, deciding to get underway and move through the water we had to ensure that the drag of the water on the limpet mine on the side of the hull wouldn't cause it to come away.

I remember going with my father in the motor boat and we trundled up and down the Ouse at different speeds with this underwater device, which nobody could see because it was under the water. And we demonstrated that the launch could travel up to 10 or 15 knots and the limpet mine was still firmly attached. So that was yet another test that my father had to undergo and it was all extremely interesting and exciting. I would repeat that this was done just before the war started.

(http://www.bbc.co.uk/ww2peopleswar/stories/34/a5961134.shtml)

The next trials were done on the River Ouse. In Alan Crawley's research into Nobby's work he stated that 'A steel plate was attached to the side of a motor boat and a limpet mine was held against it below the water line. They then went up and down the river at different speeds to find the strength of magnet that was required to hold it to a ship's hull in motion.' (Crawley, A. 'The Limpet Mine & 171-175 Tavistock Street', *BAALHS,* April 2012) John Clarke was allowed to travel in the boat and remembers being very excited by it all.

Back at the workshop, Macrae christened their new magnetic device 'The Limpet'. What they hoped was that the enemy kept their ships in good condition as it wouldn't stick to a hull covered in barnacles.

Aston House, near Stevenage, Herts. (Station XII), Radio station and later used for research, development and training in weapons and explosives. Nabby worked here during 1940.
(http://www.btinternet.com/~m.a.christie/aston.jpg)

Brickendonbury Manor (Station XVII), near Hertford where, from December 1940 — February 1942, Nobby was in charge of training SOE, OSS and other agents in the use of explosives in various kinds of industrial and other sabotage operations.
(Courtesy of Neil Rees)

The Firs, Whitchurch, near Aylesbury, Buckinghamshire (top) where Nobby worked from spring 1942 on various weaponry projects with Stuart Macrae. The workshops and hoist were at the rear. (Macrae, S. *Churchill's Toy Shop*)

The next problem they had to solve was the 'delayed action initiator'. Various types had to be devised which would detonate the limpet after a delay of anywhere between half an hour and two hours after it was stuck on the ship. As there was nothing on the market at that time, they needed

> *... a spring loaded striker, maintained in the cocked position by a pellet soluble in water. When the pellet dissolved, the striker would be released to hit a cap to initiate a detonator which would explode a primer to explode the main charge. All this was easy enough, but finding a suitable pellet was difficult. There were too many variables. The powder itself was the first one, and the degree to which it was compressed the second one. The temperature of the water made all the difference, and of course so did whether it was fresh water or sea water. Expert chemists were called in to find us the answer, but they failed. One day a pellet would dissolve at a rate that alarmed us and would no doubt have alarmed a Limpeteer. The next day, a similar one might take several hours over the job and we did not want that. There was some hope of a Limpet staying put on a stationary target and every chance of its getting washed off if the target moved off at 20 knots or so as it might well do in time.*
>
> *One of Nobby's children solved the problem for us. It was only a small one and, in sweeping it off the bench which it much preferred to its play pen, we upset it by knocking its bag of aniseed balls on to the floor. Whilst Nobby was doing the consoling act, I tried one of these sweets. It seemed to stay with me a long time, getting smaller and smaller with great regularity. After trying a couple himself Nobby agreed that this might well be the answer so we commandeered the remainder of the supply and started to experiment. I think I can safely claim to be the first man to drill holes into aniseed balls and devise a fitting to enable*

this to be done accurately and efficiently. We rigged up some of our igniters with these aniseed balls in place of soluble pellets, and the next day the children of Bedford had to go without their aniseed balls.

(Macrae, op.cit.p.9)

It must have been quite exciting for John as he recalled having to visit all the sweet shops in Bedford and purchasing all their supplies of aniseed balls. Michael Simmonds, John's friend who lived opposite on Clarendon Street, recalled playing with him in his garden.

One day, I remember, he took us into his father's factory/workshop. We were very interested, of course, and wondered why there was someone, a lady, I think, drilling holes in aniseed balls. We were told that these were for making necklaces for children to suck in hospital! We believed this and were given the crumbs from the drillings to eat. Sweet rations were short, so we were glad of a little extra! Little did we know then that the aniseed balls were really for fuses for limpet mines to be attached to enemy shipping! When the aniseed ball dissolved in the sea water, it activated the bomb.

(Communication with author, 27 March 2012)

Once the spring wire was threaded through the hole drilled through the sweet and the detonator attached, the device was immersed in water. When the aniseed ball completely dissolved, a time delay of an hour or so, the detonator would set off the explosives. This allowed the 'frogmen', saboteurs who were to attaching the limpet mines to the side of enemy ships, a safe time to escape before the charges went off. He recalled seeing

... quite a lot of this activity going on in the house, particularly this interesting development with an unusual use of aniseed balls. The aniseed balls were drilled and then they

were put into little detonator capsules and my father had these ranged around the house and setting off at different times depending on the amount of aniseed ball that was used on each detonator. He would rush into the room in the house where, on the mantlepiece, one of these charges would be put in a big glass Woolworth's tumbler and he would say, 'Right, that's 35 minutes'. It didn't matter that probably the glass had fractured and all the water had gone - he had got something that worked and they were quickly able to establish how much of an aniseed ball was needed to give the varying times of delay that the operators would require.

(http://www.bbc.co.uk/ww2peopleswar/stories/34/a5961134.shtml)

Des Turner's research into Aston House, one of SOE's requisitioned houses used for experimental work on explosives, pointed out that

The device was tested at Bletchley Park and successfully blew a hole in a barge. The next step was to try it on a moving vessel. A dummy limpet was fixed with magnets to a police launch on the Thames but it fell off, obviously the magnetic system needed to be improved.

(Turner, D. (2006), *Station XII Aston House SOE's Secret Centre*, Sutton Publishing, pp.144-45)

Between them, they came up with various improvements to their invention but, Macrae pointed out,

For safety's or danger's sake, we equipped each limpet with two of three delayed action exploders. The aniseed part of the device had of course to be protected from damp whilst it was in store - and in fact until the Limpet was actually placed on its target. So what we needed was a closed rubber sleeve of some sort which could be pushed over the tube to seal it and whipped off by the Limpeteer when the time came. Again the local shops were able to meet the requirement. We went round to the chemists buying up all their stocks of a certain commodity and earning ourselves an undeserved reputation for being sexual athletes.

(Macrae, op.cit.p.11)

During the winter of 1939 Nobby manufactured the first 250 limpets in his Tavistock Street workshop. The second order was for 1,000 so additional space was needed. He bought larger premises in Dean Street, a light industrial area of workshops and garages on the south side of Goldington Road, near the junction with Newnham Avenue.

Nobby and I had done a little costing work on Limpets. His overheads were pretty low, so the asking price came to something like £8 a time out of which he could afford to pay me £2 commission. This was probably more than the profit Nobby was making himself, but he was like that.

(Macrae, op.cit.p.20)

As knowledge of their potential spread, further orders came from not just the SOE but the Royal Marines and the OSS who were running a similar training scheme for their saboteurs. As a result of the increased demand, Bassetts, the sweet manufacturers, were given the contract to supply their aniseed balls to a company in Welwyn which was given the contract to manufacture limpets. By the time the war had ended, it had produced over half a million. Turner added that

Towards the end of the war there was an increasing demand for large quantities of limpets .a search for likely contractors revealed an agency at Elstow, Bedfordshire, that was an experimental filling unit and had no work. The problem then was how to use the unit but not their current workforce. It was eventually agreed that Aston House staff would run the plant and five or six soldiers were permanently installed there until the factory closed after VE day in 1945. they

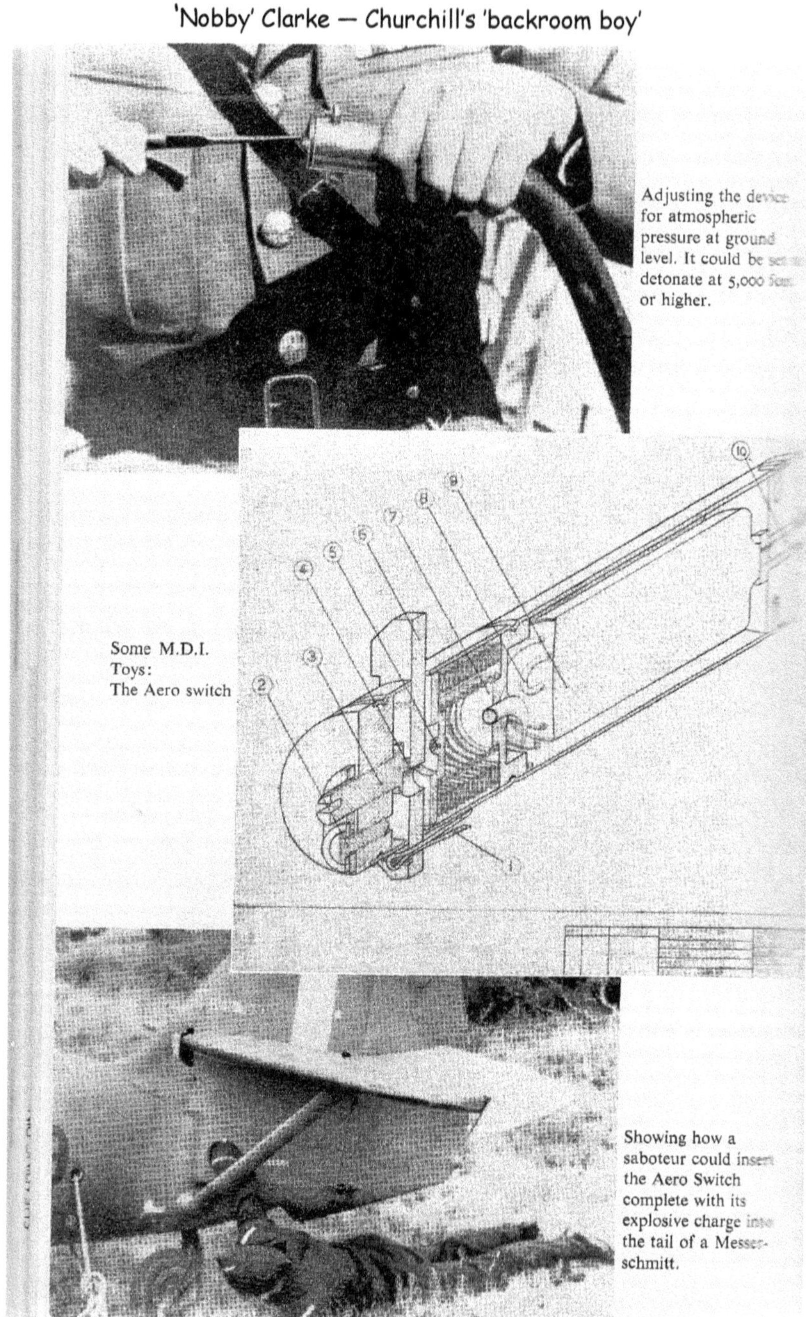

Adjusting the device for atmospheric pressure at ground level. It could be set to detonate at 5,000 feet or higher.

Some M.D.I. Toys: The Aero switch

Showing how a saboteur could insert the Aero Switch complete with its explosive charge into the tail of a Messer-schmitt.

Macrae, S. *Churchill's Toy Shop*)

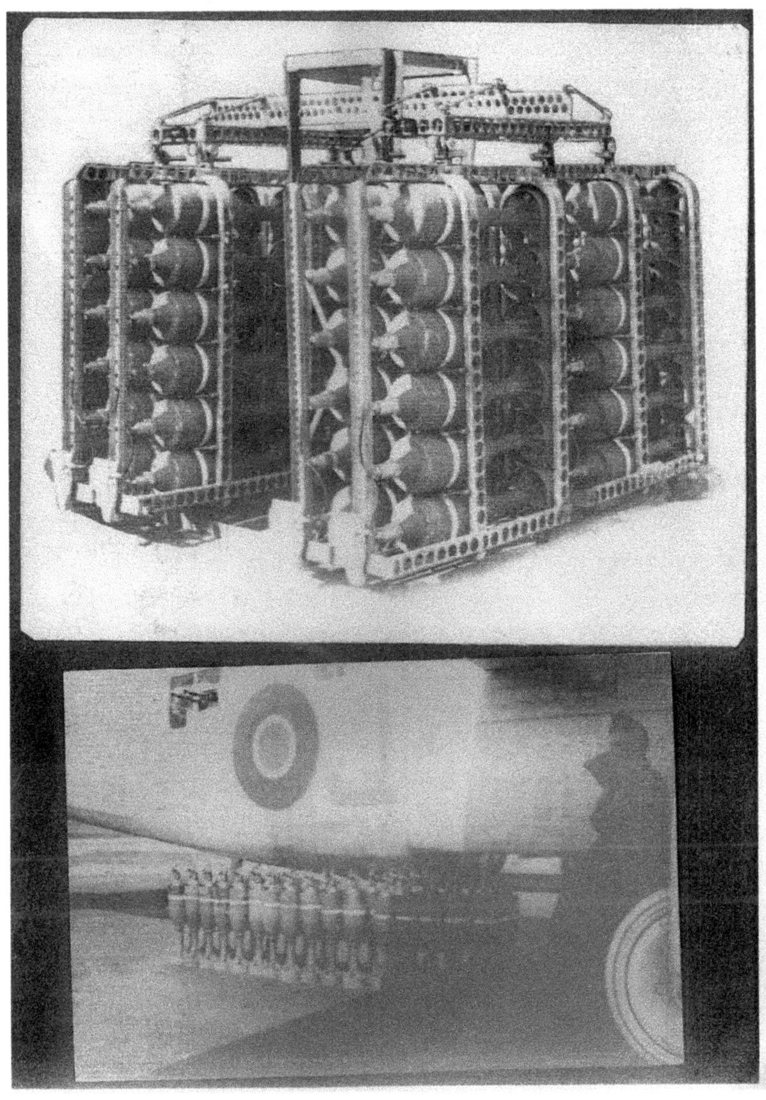

Arrangement of stowage for 48A.S. Bombs in rear bomb bay of USAAF Liberators and RAF Halifaxes. Similar stowage for an additional 24 bombs was provided in front bomb bay.
(Courtesy of Ann Clarke)

were billeted in the local firemen's accommodation, advised to be on their best behaviour and not to upset the local workers. This went well until their quarters were inspected and it was found that they had much better house-keeping and bed making services.

(Turner, op.cit.p.146)

The first use of Nobby's limpet mines was on enemy shipping near Costanza in the Danube but the major success was in Operation Frankton. On 7th December 1942 a team of ten Royal Marines, popularly known as 'The Cockleshell Heroes,' were transported in a submarine, HMS Tuna, to the mouth of the Gironde river, France. Using five, two-man canoes, they paddled by night the 70 miles upstream to the Bordeaux docks. Each man carried several limpets. The Combined Ops website narrates how

The targets were merchant ships lying in Bordeaux harbour - ships that were successfully breaking the Allied blockade particularly between Japan and Germany. Conventional methods such as bombing had been discounted. Operation Frankton was an unorthodox, imaginative and daring solution. At the end of the first night only 2 canoes and 4 men were still operational. Four nights later they inflicted damage to 5 ships lying in the harbour. Only two men survived and returned to the UK.

(http://www.combinedops.com/Cockleshell%20Heroes.htm)

Other major successes included attacks on ships in Palermo harbour in January 1943, Oslo in April 1943, Singapore in September, Portolago (Greece) and Spezia (Italy) in June 1944 and Jahore Strait (Japan) in July 1945. (Macrae, op.cit.p.221-20)

They accounted for hundreds of thousands of tons of enemy shipping and certainly this might be true if the encouraging messages we received by courtesy of our Cloak

> *and Dagger friends and heir secret radio stations were anything to go by. Time and time again we would learn that a number of enemy ships had been sunk in harbour by Limpeteers and take off our hats to those brave fellows. One such message was not so good thought. It reported that some Italians had got hold of a supply of our Limpets and to date had sunk three of our ships with them.*
>
> (Macrae, op.cit.)

During the war years, modifications were made so that Mark III had a spun aluminium bowl instead of the Woolworths' one. The horseshoe magnets were replaced with four large Alcomax magnets designed by Neill's of Sheffield and flexibly mounted so that they could attach themselves to an uneven surface. The aniseed balls were replaced by 'L' Delay fuses. A copper wire attached to the detonator was place in a capsule of weak acid. When the capsule was broken, the acid would dissolve the wire, setting off the explosive. Different strengths of acid provided different delay times. However, Macrae admitted that

> *This refined model worked no better than its primitive predecessor and oddly enough it never seemed to take on so well with the operators. Maybe this was because it was too refined. True, rubber sleeves were still used to afford initial protection to the 'L' Delays but they were now so small that they were useless for any other kind of protection.*
>
> (Ibid.)

Another weapon he was involved with was the 'Sticky Bomb' which was a grenade which could be thrown at a tank and would stick to it for five seconds or so and then explode, blowing a hole in the tank and, in Macrae's words, '*disconcert the occupants.*' There was also the 'W' Bomb, manufactured at Midgely Harmer's engineering works in the Park Royal industrial estate in Wembley, north London. It was a mine designed to be dropped by an aircraft into a river and sink to the bed and remain dormant for a predetermined period. It would then rise to just below the surface and float with the current until it came into contact with a boat or a ship whereupon it would explode with sufficient force to produce a wreck. If it failed to explode after a certain time, it would sink to the bottom and become harmless.

The 'Kangaroo Bomb' and the 'Johnnie Walker' Bomb were variants on this. Upon entering the water the bomb was expected to dive underwater then surface. This would be repeated until it struck the relatively less protected underside of a ship at which point the 90 pound Torpex warhead would explode. (http://en.wikipedia.org/wiki/MD1)

During the spring of 1940, under the direction of Colonel Grand, Royal Engineers, the head of the Secret Intelligence Service's 'D' (Destruction) Section, Nobby was involved in training potential SOE agents in the use of explosives and incendiary devices, for which he was given a commendation. Whether agents visited him in Bedford and practiced in Bedford Baths has not come to light.

Another of Clark's ideas brought him to the attention of Millis Jefferis, the founder of the Ministry of Supply's unusual weapons section. He had submitted a paper entitled "*A consideration of new offensive means*", which outlined the design of a large, high-speed trench forming machine.

In a folder in the National Archives headed MOST SECRET and underlined 'TO BE KEPT UNDER LOCK AND KEY' was a file entitled 'NAVAL LAND EQUIPMENT'. It details how, in November 1939, the First Lord of the Admiralty approached the Director of Naval Construction to construct a machine to dig trenches at the rate of 5 mph (8 kmph). Instead of large bodies of infantrymen advancing over the surface exposed to enemy fire, there was a plan for them to follow behind a machine digging a trench 7 feet (2.6m) wide and 7 feet deep, wide enough for tanks as well. A sum of £100,000 for experiments was proffered. It was hoped that 200 tank-like excavators might be available by May 1941. Brigadier King, Deputy Engineer in Chief at General Headquarters, ordered a geological survey of the countryside in the north of France and Belgium west of the Dyle River. He was asked to report on the surface and sub-surface soil and rock material down to seven feet. He identified predominantly three to four feet (1.04 - 1.48m) of loam soils or alluvium, covering beds of gravel, clay, chalk, flints, sand and shale similar to those found in Central and Southern England.

Nobby's involvement was found in a letter to the Minister headed 'SECRET'.

I have seen Major Jeffries who knows Mr. Clarke. Apparently Mr. Clarke is a man under fifty who runs a small engineering establishment at Bedford and employs 20 to 30 hands, but handles a good deal of other work by sub-contracting.

He served as a Sapper in the last War and is apparently a good practical engineer with ideas but not very deep technical knowledge. He has been vetted by M.I.5 and is considered absolutely reliable, making parts of secret machines for Major Jeffries and is at present acting as an Instructor for the training of men for very secret work for the Admiralty.

(TNA AVIA 11/2, 7th May, 1940)
)

Following an interview in which he outlined his proposals, a memo was sent to the Admiralty.

Memorandum of Interview with Mr. C. V. Clarke

Mr. Clarke called to see me by appointment this morning. I formed a very good opinion of him. he is frank, direct, obviously knowledgeable, very keen to put his whole weight into the war effort, willing to join the Department as a Temporary Civil Servant, as an Assistant Director at £1,000 a year, willing to allow any question of remuneration for proprietary rights of his inventions to remain over until

'Nobby Clarke's Churchill 'Great Eastern' with ramp erected for action with 6 feet wading extension.
(Courtesy of Ann Clarke)

Trials of the 'Great Eastern' : Top: Blast off. Middle: Bridge in position ready for tanks to make the crossing. Bottom: Recovering the section of bridge which spans the river so that another demonstration can be given. (Macrae,, S. *Churchill's Toy Shop*')

Demonstration at 'The Firs' Top: Millis Jefferis inspects the 'Great Eastern' ramp while in the background the building section completes the construction of another target.
(Macrae,, S. *Churchill's Toy Shop*')

Tank making a successful crossing using Nobby's 'Great Eastern'.
(Courtesy of Ann Clarke)

Screwing in the 'Tree Spigot' and attaching the bomb.
(Courtesy of Ann Clarke)

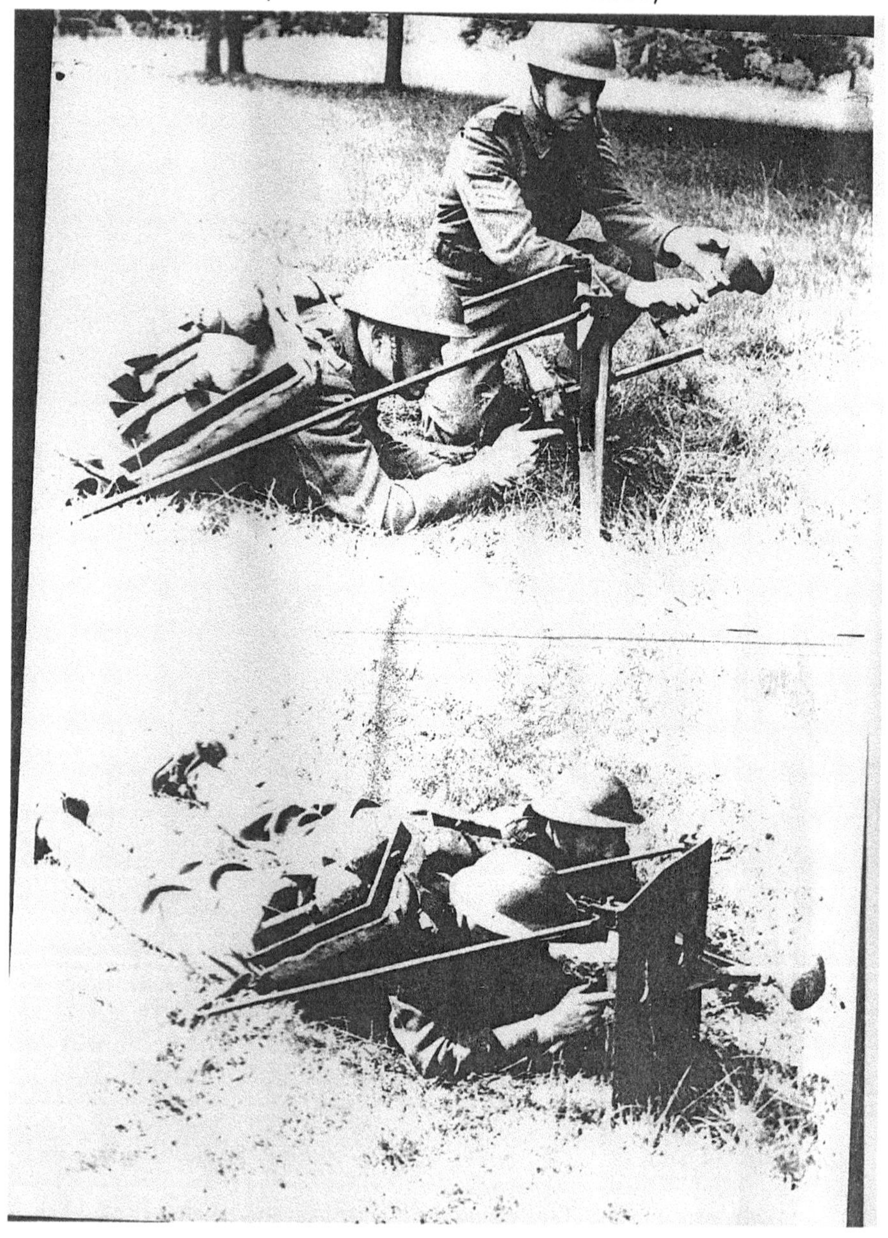

Demonstration of the 'Plate Spigot'.
(Courtesy of Ann Clarke)

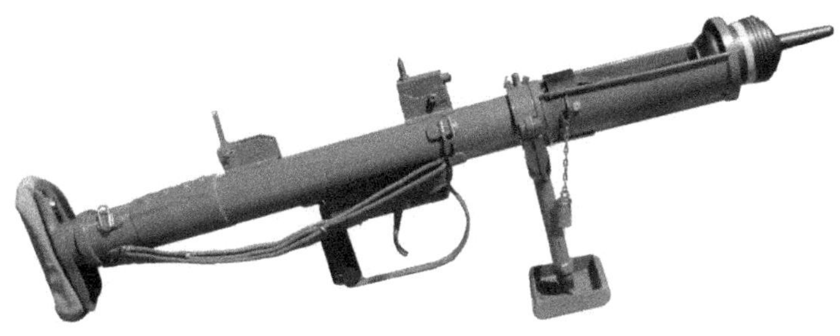

The P.I.A.T. designed by Nobby Clarke
(http://upload.wikimedia.org/wikipedia/commons/thumb/2/23/PIAT_cropped.jpg/800px-PIAT_cropped.jpg)

P.I.A.T. in action
(http://sniper07.s.n.pic.centerblog.net/ws4jkepd.jpg)

Later Limpet mine and detonator tin
http://www.millsgrenades.co.uk/images/soe/Limpet%20&%20tin.jpg

Time pencils, these were time delay detonators ranging from five minutes to several days
http://www.millsgrenades.co.uk/images/soe/SOEtime%

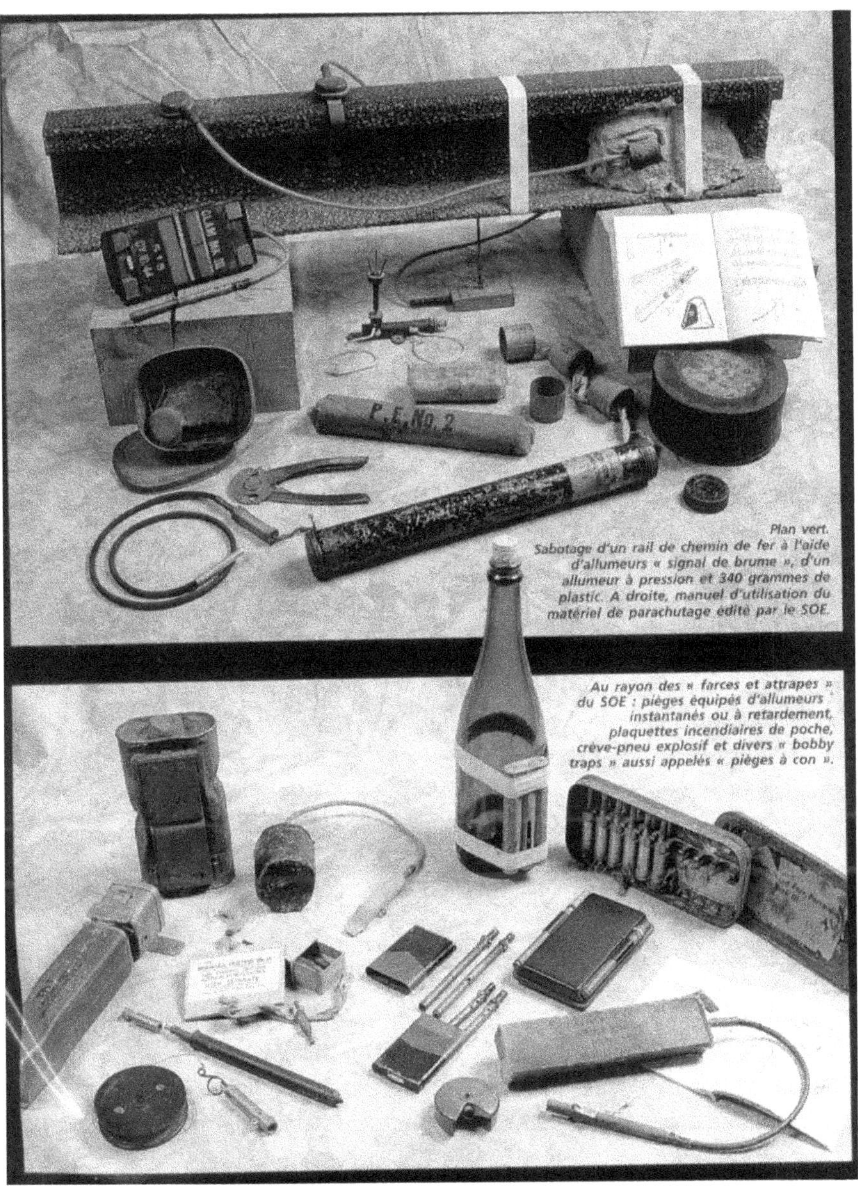

SOE's explosives kit issued to its saboteurs
http://www.millsgrenades.co.uk/images/soe/SOE_Demolition_Display_Pic01.jpg

after the war, does not think that any organisation with which he is connected would be an appropriate one for manufacturing his machine, and understands that the machine would be developed and worked out by us as a Department, free of expense to himself.

I subsequently called in Mr. Hopkins and Mr. McBain, and went over the interview again with Mr. Clarke. Mr. Clarke is to reflect on whether he wishes to bring any staff with him, and whether there are any models for which any remuneration ought to be paid, and will let us have an answer probably by the end of the current week.

Mr. Clarke is 43 years of age. He is connected with the Low Loading Trailer Company, Limited. D.A. Clarke, who signs some of his private letters, is his wife. We are dealing with an individual, and not with a company, partnership, or association. Mr. Clarke is accustomed to secret work, and has access to a special naval school, where certain experiments have been carried out by him. Mr. Clarke is prepared to sign the Official Secrets Act. He was good enough to say that he felt that the interview had been carefully prepared, that all the points which he would desire to have raised had been covered, that he entirely understands the proposal that was being made to him, and had no other points which he in his turn desired to raise at this stage. In answer to Mr. Hopkins, he said that he would be quite prepared, if it were so desired, to take out a secret patent for his invention.

(TNA AVIA 11/2, 8th May, 1940)

Winston Churchill, supported his proposals., describing him as 'a man of remarkable coincidences of ideas,' As a result, in May 1940, he was appointed Assistant Director, Naval Land Section, Ministry of Supply, with a salary of £1,000 a year. Under the directorship of Mr. Hopkins, Naval Constructor, his job was to complete the design and construction of these 60 feet long machines. The weight of each machine was 140 tons, and the proposed performance was the capacity to advance through the Siegfreid Line, heavily defended German defences running north-south along the their border with Holland, Belgium and France. Nobby's plan was that it laid and fired explosive charges in front of itself so that it could make much quicker progress. He expected it to travel at 200 yards per hour and progress three to four miles in a night. The trench it formed, up to 10 feet wide and 8 feet deep, was big enough to accommodate tanks. A long artillery would be needed during its operation to drown out its noise. Plans were made to build a prototype but on 25th June 1940, France's General Petain surrendered to the Germans, which meant the target disappeared and the scheme was shelved.

He immediately resigned from the Ministry of Supply and notified the War Office of his availability. Called up almost immediately, he signed the Official Secrets Act and was posted to the Intelligence Corps for special duty and joined the SOE staff at their Technical Research and Development Station at Aston House (Station XII), near Stevenage, Hertfordshire.

Aston House was a large country house, set in a secluded five-acre park thirty miles (48km) north of London and only a short drive from Knebworth railway station. It had been requisitioned by the Special Intelligence Services, the covert section of the Foreign Office, in 1939 but was taken over by the SOE. A pond and large chalk pit were used for testing explosives. Bickham Sweet-Escott, an SOE officer, mentioned Aston House in his wartime memoirs, *Baker Street Irregular*.

> *Its first commandant was Arthur Langley, a naval commander who won a Victoria Cross and his staff engaged in the design, testing and production of explosives and secret weapons for use in sabotage operations and guerrilla warfare.*

In Des Turner's book *Station XII,* he described the park as being surrounded by a high wire fence and the locals being told that it was being used to test aircraft flares, special rockets for the Navy and special star-shell fillings for the Army. Staff wore old civilian clothes,, always wore sunglasses and were introduced by fictitious names.

When Nobby first arrived at Aston House 'to sort out a little problem with the Limpet mine,' he did not create a very good impression with his superiors. Macrae mentioned that

> *Nobby never did stand on ceremony. After waiting five minutes or so at the Guard Post he wandered off and contrived to avoid all security measures and get himself into the house and Langley's presence in another five minutes flat. Nobby relished this kind of exercise and specialised in it later on when he joined the Cloak and Dagger experts himself - first at this station E.S.6* [Experimental Station] *and later as O.C.* [Officer in Command] *of one at Hertford. But although Langley belonged to the same Senior Service he would not wear this one at all. Next day I received a note from him deploring the conduct on behalf of an officer for whom I was responsible. In future, he said, would I please send some officer with some sense of responsibility to Aston House on these missions. If I again sent Captain Clarke he might be admitted to the grounds of Aston House to carry out such work as the testing of Limpets but in no circumstances would he be allowed inside the house and he could not be served with meals. Langley went off a few months later to take a more active part in the war at sea and Nobby then did get into the house for meals. In fact he lived there for several months, having been taken on the strength by Commander Langley's successor - Captain L.J.C. Wood.*
>
> (Macrae, op.cit.p.94)

Whilst stationed there, agents were also taught the art of silent killing by two ex-Shanghai policemen, Fairburn and Sykes, whose talents were eventually recognised by the OSS who had them transferred to teach their agents in Whitby, Canada. Whether Nobby picked up a few skills from them before they left is unknown.

Turner quoted Major Wood detailing how

> *We invented, made, supplied and trained personnel in the use of 'toys' not only for the resistance but for all the special forces: Commandoes, Small Boat Section, Airborne Division and Long Range Desert Patrol. We had about forty specialised army officers and civilians, guards and several hundred soldiers, FANYs and ATS (First Aid Nursing Yeomanry and Auxiliary Transport Service—the women's services; by WWII FANY had no nursing connections0 and a few civilian technicians. We had magazines for explosives, and sheds in which to handle them and large storehouses for incendiaries and all the rest of our 'toys', and workshops wherein to experiment and manufacture. We designed and made up special explosive charges tailored for the job in hand and simple to place and fire by any commando or resistance worker. Many tons of explosives as well as devices we supplied were dropped by parachute to the resistance to blow bridges on D-Day. The whole essence of helping the special forces was speed in both invention and supply.*
>
> (Turner, D. (2006), *Station XII Aston House SOE's Secret Centre*, Sutton, pp.8-9)

When he was not demonstrating or developing explosives, Nobby wrote the 'Blue Book', a manual used by SOE on sabotage technique. Included were instructions on how to use a new light weapon he had invented and produced prototypes for. The existing mortar firing gun had such powerful recoil, his modifications so improved its effectiveness that the Americans purchased large quantities of his 'Tree Spigot'. Their Field Photographic Unit produced an instructional film for OSS agents in which it told them that

> *The spigot gun was a booby trap or saboteurs weapon for attack against both moving and stationary and moving targets. It is very light and portable and capable of throwing a comparatively heavy bomb with accuracy up to 250 yards. The equipment for spigot gun operation consists of the spigot, the base of the gun, sights for aiming the gun and the bomb which is projected at the target. The spigot has an augur-like handle for setting into the tree or other substantial support and one of the handles is chiselled for scraping away bark. The spigot rod is mounted in the base in a ball and socket joint so it may be aimed and elevated as required. A clamp holds it firmly in the aimed position. The rod contains a spring actuated striker which is held in cocked position by the end of a trip wire inserted in the hole between rod and striker. The sight, similar in principle to a view finder on a camera has range scales in both metres and yards. It fits on the spigot rod while the operator centres the gun on the target before the bomb is attached. The bomb which sits over the spigot rod and is projected to the target is made up of three parts - tail, head and fuse. In the tail there is a shot-gun type of cartridge which when hit by the firing pin of the spigot rod supplies the driving force of the bomb. The silencing rod keeps gases, flames and smoke inside the tail of the bomb making the point of firing very difficult to locate. When the striker in the spigot rod is released by removing the trip wire it springs forward to hit the cartridge in the bomb tail. The exploding cartridge drives the bomb off the rod and the silencing rod and shell peel themselves in the end of the tail preventing the escape of noise and fire. The initial acceleration arms the special fuse so that when the*

> *bomb hits its target the impact drives the fuse firing pin into a detonating cap which ignites the booster charge. This booster charge in turn detonates the three pounds of plastic explosive carried in the bomb head.*
>
> (http://www.realmilitaryflix.com/public/253.cfm)

Time pencils could be inserted when the saboteur felt that they did not need to be present when the vehicle, locomotives, oil storage tanks or building was hit. His 'Plate Spigot' was the same but attached to the gun was a bullet-proof steel plate which screened the firer. Both these weapons were taken on by E.S.6, the War Office as they could also be used by the Home Guard should an invasion ever take place. He also designed a light, portable explosive road trap which was successfully used by SOE and OSS agents. Exactly what it was, was not specified but to give you an idea, the SOE's 'backroom boys' concealed explosives in cavities inside actual everyday objects or in life-size replicas made of plaster or celluloid. These included exploding rusty nuts and bolts, wooden clogs, Chianti wine bottles, screw-top milk bottles, fountain pens, railway fishplates, oilcans, lifebelts, bicycle pumps, food tins, candles, soap, shaving brushes, books, loaves of bread, lumps of coal, rock, turnips, beetroots, stuffed mice and rats and even cow, horse, mule and camel dung!

In December 1940 he was promoted to Captain (Acting Major) and appointed Officer in Charge (O.C.) of Brickendonbury Manor (Station XVII), near Hertford. This was a special school used for the assembly, final training and dispatch of operational parties; the training of SOE staff for missions abroad and special training in industrial and railway sabotage. Frank Gleason, an OSS agent, reported how he was sent to an industrial sabotage school in England run by the SOE.

> *Six or seven people that are properly trained can cripple a good-sized city. It's as easy as can be. These*

> *terrorists scare me. If they know this stuff, which I'm sure they do, it's really easy to cripple a medium-sized city with trained demolitionists and arsonists. We learned how to operate and destroy locomotives and power plants, the turbines in power plants, communication systems, and telephones. We also learned how to make people sick by poisoning the city's water supply. Shitty stuff like that - we were taught to fight dirty.*
>
> *Using a locomotive we learned how to take the controls and get the train moving at a high speed, and jump off - creating a runaway train that would plow into something - isn't that awful? We destroyed rolling stock by removing grease in the gearboxes and putting sugar in gasoline tanks to destroy the engines. We learned how to make explosives from sugar, from basic household supplies, how to start a fire that could take out a city.*
>
> (McDonnell, P.K. (2004), *Operatives, Spies and Saboteurs,* Citadel Press, p.7)

According to John, his father felt it very important that these enthusiastic foreign volunteers should get some actual hands on experience of trying to carry out an attack.

> *So my father made out a pass on War Office paper saying: 'The holder of this pass, Major C. V. Clarke, has authority to inspect Luton Power Station.' So armed with this pass, which I'm sure from judging the signature which looked remarkably like my father's, he took his team from Hertford to Luton one dark night. They used scaling ladders to get over the walls of Luton Power Station, which of course was guarded like all big installations. They successfully got inside, planted dummy charges on all the transformers, then got back over the wall successfully without anybody noticing. They, having cleared off to a nearby street and waited for my father who then walked up to the front door of the power station which of course was under guard and asked for the Officer of the guard*

and produced his pass and he said, 'I want to do a routine inspection.' So he went round with a very big torch and he came up to the first transformer and he flashed his torch and he said, 'What's that?' And this young Subaltern who was in charge of the guard, 'I'm not quite sure what this is Sir.' 'It looks to me like an explosive charge. Let's have a look round.' And in the end the poor Subaltern in charge of the guard was knocked kneed with what he'd let happen. So my father, who was a kindly man said, 'Alright old man, you say nothing about this and I'll say nothing about it. But you've learnt your lesson.' With that he had his team back to retrieve the appliances and off they went. But this was very valuable training, slightly unorthodox but it's one of those things that happened in war time. One of the more wilder outfits in the Army during the war!

(http://www.bbc.co.uk/ww2peopleswar/stories/51/a5961251.shtml)

It was common for SOE officers to undertake the same training as the agents. Accordingly, in June 1941, Nobby was sent to Manchester where he attended a parachute course at Ringway Aerodrome. This usually involved five days learning how to jump from increasing heights, land and roll without hurting oneself, put on ankle supports, padded clothing and a sorbo rubber hat, attach the harness and parachute and then make practice three jumps from an air balloon at about 500 feet before two from a converted Whitley Bomber over the nearby Tatton Park. One was at night.

Whilst at Ringway he had an accident which Major Edwards, the Station Commandant, reported on.

I was present on the ground quite near this officer, when he made a descent by parachute, landed rather heavily, and remained on the ground until I came to him with the Medical Officer, who immediately examined the ankle. He was able to walk to the car, and received proper medical treatment.

He was on duty at the time, and no personal blame can be attached to him.

(TNA HS 9 /321.8)

Three of the agents he taught were flown out of RAF Tempsford on the night of 11th/12th May. Group Captain Hockey and S/L Jackson flew a Whitley to Bordeaux on operation JOSEPHINE. Captain A. Forman, R. P. Calard and Lt. Varnier were parachuted on a mission to blow up the Pessac power station. On reconnoitring the transformer station, they couldn't get past the guards, the 9 ft (2.7 m) wall and the high-tension wire. They also failed to make contact with the submarine which attempted to pick them up on the 20th May. Not to be outdone, they lay low for a month, used specialist gear to climb the wall, open the main gate and set their charges. Six of the eight transformers were blown up. The charges slipped off the other two before exploding and the party escaped.

The disruption to the Bordeaux area took the Germans a long time to recover from. 250 people were reported as arrested, the Pessac area was fined 1,000,000 French Francs and 12 German sentries were shot. Michael Foot, the SOE historian, commented that Mr H.B. Dalton, the Minister of Economic Warfare, contacted Churchill about the importance of the JOSEPHINE mission.

We may therefore take it as practically certain that three trained men, dropped from one aeroplane, have succeeded in destroying an important industrial target. This strongly suggests that many industrial targets, especially if they cover only a very small area, are more effectively attacked by SOE methods than by air bombardment... I hope that with the cooperation of the RAF we shall be able to repeat this form of attack during the coming autumn and winter.

(Foot, M.R.D. (1999), The Special Operations Executive 1940 -1946, Pimlico, London)

Whether Churchill acknowledged Nobby's contribution is unknown. John Clarke added that the power station supplied nearby 'U' boat pens from where German submarine left on operations to attack Allied convoys out in the Atlantic. Putting them out of action for several months whilst the power station was being repaired was a major contribution to the war effort. (http://www.bbc.co.uk/ww2peopleswar/stories/97/a4372797.shtml).

In the summer of 1941 Nobby designed and fitted concealed Spigot guns to a Brixham trawler which was used in SOE operations off the African coasts. Two months after being promoted Temporary Major, in December 1941 he handed over command of Station XVII and joined SOE Headquarters staff as the Officer in Charge of user trials of special arms and equipment.

Another measure of his and Colonel Wood's success at Brickendonbury were the careful planning of SOE missions. Perhaps the most famous was carried out by two Czechoslovakian soldiers, Jan Kubiš and Josef Gabčik. After training using Nobby's newly invented blast grenade on a slow-moving Austin in the grounds of Aston House, they were taken to the airfield. Perhaps there were no flights available at Tempsford that night as they were driven from London to RAF Tangmere, an airfield on the south coast near Christchurch. Their mission was to assassinate Reinhard Heydrich, the Nazi governor of Czechoslovakia, in June 1942. Turner related how

> *The device was a modified British No. 73 Anti-Tank Grenade. The standard grenade had a tin plate body 9.5 in long and 3.25 in diameter containing 3.25 lbs of Polar Ammon Gelatin Dynamite, a nitro-glycerine-based explosive. The grenade was fitted with the No. 247 fuse made of black bakelite which is often referred to as the 'all ways fuse' designed to function on impact irrespective of how the grenade landed. Total weight was 4 lb. However, the*

grenades that Jan Kubiš had to carry were a conversion of the standard grenade made from the upper third portion only. The filling was prevented from falling out by covering the open end with adhesive tape and then binding the whole with tape for added security. The effect of the conversion was to cut the size and the weight to just over 1 lb which would make the device easier to throw and conceal.

[...] *there was no limit to the amount of preparation the agents could be given, and it was recognised during the planning of the attack that they would have to seize any opportunity that presented itself . Consequently they took a positive arsenal of weaponry with them including: 2 Colt 0.38 Supers (with shoulder holsters), 4 spare magazines, 100 rounds of ammunition, 4 percussion bombs with PE* [plastic explosive], *2 detonator magazines, 2 Mills bombs, (4-second fuses), 1 tree spigot mortar, 1 coil trip wire, 2 igniters, 1 spigot bomb, 1 4-hour time delay fuse for use with 2-lb PE charge, 3 electric detonators and 30 inches of wire and battery, 1 Sten gun, 100 rounds of ammunition, 32 lb PE, 10 lb gelignite, 2 yards of cordtex, 4 fog signals, 3 time pencils, 1 lethal hypodermic syringe.*

(Turner, D. (2006), *Station XII Aston House, SOE's Secret Centre*, Sutton Publishing,p.110)

Nobby was also involved in training the agents who undertook the November 1942 attack on Oran harbour in Algeria, where the French Fleet was sunk to avoid it falling into German hands, and in 1943, the destruction of the Norsk-Hydro 'heavy water' plant at Vermork, Rjukan, in Norway. It stopped the Germans from producing a nuclear bomb.

When Flying Fortresses and Lancaster bombers failed to halt production at the Renault engineering works in Lyon that was producing armoured vehicles for the German military, Harry Rée, an SOE agent, trained by Nobby, successfully brought it to a standstill with a few carefully placed explosives. In Harry's interview held at the Imperial War Museum, he recalled that

> *The first sabotage was about the beginning of November and they decided they'd blow up a whole transformer house where all the electricity came into the factory. About five men were involved, Frenchmen who worked in the factory. They had their pistols in the pockets of their overalls and they had their explosives, plastic blocks with room for a detonator, in their pockets too. There was a wonderful carelessness about the whole thing. They were playing football with the German guards outside the transformer house—somebody had forgotten to get the key—and in playing football one of them dropped his plastic block of explosive and one of the German guards who was playing football pointed it out to him. 'You've dropped something, sir, I think.' he put it back in his pocket. That was absolutely typical. The transformer house blew up and after they went on throughout the whole of the rest of the war fixing these magnetic blocks to machines and enormously reducing production.*
>
> (IWM 8688/2; 8720/3)

The Dunlop tyre factory in Montluçon was similarly disabled in 1944 using two pounds of explosives. Two of Nobby's colleagues who also worked at Brickendonbury were Guy Burgess, and Kim Philby, later discovered to have been working for the Soviet Union. One wonders what sort of report they gave their Russian masters about Nobby. It was Burgess who came up with the idea of setting up a school for training agents and Philby, his friend from their days at Cambridge University, drew up the syllabus. (O'Connor, B. (2013) *Churchill's School for Saboteurs: Station XVII)*, Amberley Publishing

Amongst the nationalities John recalled his father helping were Poles, French and Dutch. Sometimes he providing them with a brief respite from their training.

I remember as an example of my father's trust in me because I had an uncle who had a farm out at Pulloxhill in Bedfordshire. My father, shortly before an operation was due to take place and before a group of saboteurs were sent off, they having been trained up to the limit and needing a couple of days' break, were sent by my father across to Pulloxhill to help bring in the harvest or do some other job on the farm and it happened that I was there at the same time. My father told me that these foreign people who were on the farm helping my uncle, were saboteurs, that they were going to be dropped over Europe but they were not to know under any circumstances that I was Major Clarke's son. So we kept absolutely quiet about that and worked with them in the field as they were having their break before going on their dangerous missions.

(http://www.bbc.co.uk/ww2peopleswar/stories/15/a5961215.shtml)

In February 1942, Nobby requested a transfer to M.D.I. Ministry of Supply, in order to finalise the development and production of his latest sabotage device known as the 'Altimeter Switch'. Nobby visited Macrae at the Firs in Whitchurch, near Aylesbury, Buckinghamshire, another of SOE's requisitioned properties and described as

... an ideal place for us. The large house could provide both offices and sleeping accommodation. There was extensive stabling, which could readily be converted into workshops. There were several cottages on the premises and, best of all, included in the property were levelled sites where buildings to serve as stores and so forth could be erected. There were also fields which could be used as firing ranged and where experimental demolition work could be carried out

... What was wanted was a small sabotage device which could be inserted into a German bomber by some brave fellow and would explode when the aircraft reached a

certain height and cripple it ... Nobby Clarke's contribution to this sabotage device was to insist that it should have a flexible sausage of explosive ... In this instance he had worked out that such a weapon as this could not be conveniently concealed in the pocket but could without comment be carried in the trousers. He was wrong about the 'without comment' and there was always considerable ribaldry when he demonstrated this method to his pupils. But actually it was sound common sense and I believe they all adopted it.

In due course we went into production at Whitchurch with this Aero Switch and made and issued many thousands of them. Later by special request we managed to get the operational height down to 5,000 feet without sacrificing the saboteur's safety. The usual drill was to make a slit in the wing fabric of a German bomber and pop this thing inside so that in due course the wing would be wrecked

(Macrae, op.cit.p.88, 155-6)

It was successfully used in numerous SOE operations. After signing the Official Secret Act again, he was appointed Assistant Superintendent and in May 1942, when M.D.I. became a Directorate, its Deputy Assistant Director.

During this time he acted as a Liaison Officer with Imperial Chemicals Industries Limited at their works in Ardeer, in Scotland and Billingham, County Durham. They were involved in the design and manufacture of high explosives and the filling of shells and mortars. One of their inventions which was of interest to Nobby was

... a little 1.7 grain detonator which was only about the size of a percussion cap but instead of needing a blow of 3in/lb to set it off only had to be prodded lightly with a needle point.

(Macrae, op.cit.p.56)

These were used in the 'Clam', a much smaller and more portable version of the Limpet. Macrae claimed that it was their second best seller and that,

> *For the Cloak and Dagger boys it was God's Gift from Heaven. They could carry these things in their pockets and just stick them to something they would like to blow up. although the explosive content was only around 8 ounces, ICI produced some very high speed stuff for us and the design was such that the explosive was almost in contact with the target over a considerable area. A Clam could put any motor vehicle out of commission or an aero engine for that matter. But its success was dependant on the use of the 'L' Delay which was made part of it. If operators had had to use it with a Time Pencil they would not have been so enthusiastic about it. My diary is full of notes of people squealing for Clams. The Russians had nearly a million of them and were always asking for more. The total number of Clams made under M.D.I. surveillance during the war was over two and a half million.*
>
> (Macrae,op.cit.p.155)

Macrae used them to produced what he called 'M'-Mines, small explosive devices which he was able to produce at five shillings (£0.25) a time. The ICI detonators were also used in shells designed for another of Nobby's projects, the design and development of the projector for the 'Projector, Infantry, Anti-Tank (P.I.A.T) gun. Although he designed a silencing attachment for the propellant cartridge, the Director General did not consider this necessary when the weapon was used by regular troops.

> *It consisted of a steel tube, a trigger mechanism and firing spring, and was based on the spigot mortar system; instead of using a propellant to directly fire a round, the*

> *spring was cocked and tightened. When the trigger was pulled, it released the spring which pushed the spigot forward into the rear of the bomb. This detonated the propellant in the bomb itself, which was then thrown forward off the spigot. It possessed an effective range of approximately 100 yards (90 m).*
>
> *This system meant that the PIAT had several advantages, which included a lack of muzzle smoke to reveal the position of the user, the ability to fire it from inside buildings, and an inexpensive barrel; however, this was countered by, amongst other things, a difficulty in cocking the weapon, the bruising the user received when firing it, and problems with its penetrative power.*
>
> (http://en.wikipedia.org/wiki/PIAT)

Another of his designs was an auto-release frame system for dropping closely-spaced sticks of small contact bombs from the American Liberator aircraft. This gear was for use with the 35 lb A/S bomb developed by the D.M.D.I. He acted as Liaison Officer with Coastal Command for operational trials. These included 100 hours operational flying with No. 224 squadron based then in Ulster in Northern Ireland and he was involved in one successful attack. With the success of this equipment, he went on to design a similar type of release gear for the Halifax aircraft which were dropping containers of supplies for the resistance movements. (Clarke's Military Record P141671)

John described his father's new posting at

> *... a Special Weapon Developments Station set up by Professor Lindemann who became Lord Cherwell, who was Churchill's chief scientific advisor. By this time of course Churchill was Prime Minister and also Churchill had made himself Minister of Defence. The one establishment under the Ministry of Defence that he set up was this research and development weapon station situated just north of Aylesbury in the village of Whitchurch which was code*

named MD1 Whitchurch, Ministry of Defence 1. My father became Deputy Assistant Director of this secret station where his former colleague Stuart Macrae was already installed and was in fact Second in Command of the outfit there. It became a very, very big and important enterprise because the great thing about MD1 Whitchurch, which was Commanded by Colonel Jeffries, a Regular Royal Engineer Officer of great distinction.

The thing that made their work different from that of the Regular Army and Ministry of Defence weapon procurement sections was that they had no time whatsoever for red tape. They got things done at twice or thrice perhaps the speed at which the normal procurement method of designing and getting things into production would take. They weren't always terribly popular with some of the Regular Army people who had been doing the job all their Army careers, but they did achieve some very great results.

When my father was in MD1 Whitchurch he was of course carrying on with his weapon development and he devised a system for attacking U boats by air using Liberator aircraft which were used in the later part of the war. It was one of many different types of approach to destroying the German submarines which sailed out of the west coast of France into the Atlantic. His particular contribution was a 35 lb. armour piercing bomb which is quite a small bomb but the thing was that, rather than dropping one or two large bombs from an aircraft at a very small target of a submarine which is rapidly trying to disappear below the waves, it consisted of 20 or 30 smaller charges which were dropped in a scatter device so that they covered a much larger area. Therefore they were more likely to get one of these bombs attacking and actually hitting the target.

My father was attached to Coastal Command for several months flying up and down from St. Eval aerodrome in

Cornwall down to Gibraltar and back again in the Liberators and they achieved one or two sinkings as a result of their activities.

One of the chief benefits as far as we children were concerned was we found that my father coming home at weekends from Aylesbury - he occasionally managed to get back to Bedford for a night or two, bearing gifts of bananas and oranges which were totally unknown at that time of the war.

(http://www.bbc.co.uk/ww2peopleswar/stories/15/a5961215.shtml)

Training saboteurs, according to Macrae,

... was just Nobby's cup of tea and enabled him to become a bigger menace than ever. He had no guards on the gates of his magnificent estate. One just drove in and then found the vehicle being battered by rounds fired by spigot mortars set off by trip wires. Nobby would emerge smiling and point out that if they had been live rounds the occupants of the vehicles would no longer be in this world. But that was little consolation to the driver who had to explain how the bodywork of his vehicle had been badly bashed.

Nobby made a hobby of raiding the local RAF and transformer stations, leaving his dummy charges all over the place, and then ringing up the fellow in charge to point out that his security measures were lousy. This made him unpopular, and although Colin Gubbins [Head of SOE] *liked him he felt that he might be of more use elsewhere.*

(Macrae, op.cit.p.195)

During the winter of 1943 he visited various weapon training schools and Eighth Army units in North Africa, Italy, Egypt and Palestine to demonstrate the use of the P.I.A.T. and the new 426 fuze to replace the 425 fuze. Whilst in Italy he wrote a rude sonnet on the River Po and

> *... fell foul of the D of A's representative who was a Brigadier and came home with his tail between his legs. Thoroughly disgruntled, he retired hurt to his Bedford home without bothering to tell anyone that he was back and I had quite a job to get him out of a Court Martial on grounds of desertion.*
>
> *After finding a little excitement by going out in Sunderland flying boats from St Eval to see what happened when they dropped our anti-submarine bombs, Nobby returned to The Firs where I tried hard to find him suitable work without much success. When he thought up an idea for a rocket-operated tank bridge it was a great relief to me. It seemed most unlikely the thing would work but developing it would get Nobby out of my hair for a while. So I got* [Sir] *Millis* [Jefferis - *his C.O.] to approve the project.*
>
> *It was quite an impressive one, calling for many men and much equipment. But by now we were quite influential, and I had no difficulty at all in getting a couple of Churchill tanks complete with drivers right away. Nobby got to work, hardly pausing for sleep, and quickly produced some sketches which some genius at G. A. Harvey Ltd of Greenwich managed to translate into masses of girderwork. Large lorries brought this heavy gear to Whitchurch and after we had armed the workshop staff with much bigger spanners they made something of it.*
>
> *Came the day when Nobby was prepared to demonstrate his creation to one and all. It was a kind of Bailey Bridge carried on the back of a Churchill tank in a folded up position. The idea was that on reaching a canal or narrow river that must be crossed the tank driver halted on the brink of the bank and pressed Button A. This resulted in rockets being fired to throw over the folded*

part of the contrivance to form a bridge over which tanks could run.

As the pioneer, Nobby of course insisted on being the presser of Button A and nobody else wanted the job anyway. Unfortunately he had not consulted Millis about the mathematics of this venture and had just installed some 3" rockets to make sure the bridge was thrown over. It was, and it very nearly took the Churchill with it. The driver of the tank was not in a good shape but Nobby remained unshaken and signalled to the driver of another Churchill tank and a Sherman tank who were standing by to climb over his bridge. This the brave fellows did and the viability of Nobby's project was proven.

The rockets were tamed, and quite quickly Nobby's 'Great Eastern' became one of our show pieces. We used to poop it off and send tanks of all shapes and sizes over it. The big brass loved this, and I had a lot of fun devising means for recovering the bridge reasonably quickly ready for the next demonstration [...] *In due course, the first ten Great Easterns were completed and Nobby accompanied them to France after D-Day. They were used and did good work, but unfortunately they were a bit late in the day. If they could have been made available in hundreds it would have made a lot of difference.*

(Macrae, op.cit.pp.196-7)

His son added that, when the rockets were fired, the upper part lifted 60 feet into the air and that it could be used to cross 12 feet high concrete walls or 30 feet wide rivers or canals.

In the spring of 1944 he commenced the development of the 3rd Mortar jumping ammunition and its fuze which gave a low air burst, a service requirement. He also designed another new type of mortar bomb for air burst ammunition. This was fitted with a high grade explosive and had a manipulated steel tubular body and outer wire winding.

Another idea was a self-propelled multiple mortar firing device for the A43 Churchill tank, known as 'The Black Prince' manufactured by Vauxhall motors. The 17 pounder (76 mm) gun had a maximum rate of fire of 60 rounds a minute.

Whilst his father was engaged in this top secret work, John was kept busy with various cycling adventures. Maybe Nobby joined in on some of them.

finally in 1944 we went to a much more interesting place in many ways, which was Ledbury in Herefordshire where we were again harvesting but this time plum harvesting and apple harvesting from the fruit crops in the area. These were school parties that were taken out and we camped and had a wonderful time working in the orchards during the day and trying not to get to badly stung by wasps and relaxing in the evenings going out for walks in the beautiful countryside there. So these were really the main holidays that were organised.

But again as I reached the age of about 15 or 16 we used our cycles a great deal. All our 'day boys' in Bedford had cycles because it was very much a town full of cyclists, far more than today. We used to go on holiday with tents and on one occasion, the first time in 1944, we, I and a friend in the Upper School, in September of 1944 we cycled from Bedford up through the Fens to Kings Lynn. And then round the Norfolk coast down as far as into Suffolk and as far as Aldeburgh. I remember the joy of having our first swim in the sea after five years, in Cromer. And another one at Happisburgh a few miles down the coast where you could bathe on a hundred yard stretch between the mined sections of the beaches. As long as you didn't stray, you were alright. On the way back through the beautiful Suffolk countryside we saw the most remarkable sight which was hosts and hosts of gliders being towed for the Arnhem landings in Holland. We didn't know where they were going but it was obvious that there was an extraordinarily large operation taking place. [This was Operation MARKET GARDEN on September 17th, 1944.] *We cycled along with our heads in the air, likely to bump into other things because we were constantly looking up to see another team of planes with gliders behind them, hundreds and hundreds of gliders over this Sunday morning. The whole session took three or four hours to pass and it really was an extremely memorable sight.*

Then also the following year with a party of about three other school friends we cycled all the way round Wales. Going from Bedford to the Severn up through wild Wales, up the course of the Wye up to near Snowdon. We then climbed Snowdon, going inadvertently across a live firing range which we didn't really realise it was until we came back again and found that the place that we had crossed at the foot of the mountain was littered with cartridges. Then cycling back through North Wales in beautiful weather and then through the lovely orchard country of Worcestershire and back to Bedford."

http://www.bbc.co.uk/ww2peopleswar/stories/52/a5961152.shtml

Before the war ended his Great Easterns had come off the production line and been shipped to Holland.

My father went out and trained Canadians in the 21st Army Group in the spring of 1945 by which time all the trials had taken place, to use in the latter stages of the war in Holland. The particular use where they felt it could be used was on canals. He trained the Canadians up to a

high degree and they were all ready to go to use the bridges across canals, because within 30 seconds or so of the bridge being launched tanks could follow up and cross the bridge and get across what otherwise would be an unfordable obstacle. To my father's private disgust and disappointment, it was ready and planned to carry out an operation at the end of April 1945 when the Germans put their hands up in the Low Countries and the operation was therefore called off.

(http://www.bbc.co.uk/ww2peopleswar/stories/51/a5961251.shtml)

During the war Churchill's 'backroom boys', like Nobby, generated a wide range of weaponry and gadgets but he deserves credit for coming up with so many ideas and developing them. Released from Army Service on 1st November 1945, he went back to Bedford. The family moved to 65 Putnoe Lane and he joined the Territorial Army as Captain for a year before transferring to the Intelligence Corps.

In 1953 the Royal Commission gave him a £300 award for his 'Air Pressure Switch', £400 for his 'Magnetic Bomb (Limpet), but only acknowledged his Magnetic Time Bomb (Clam)' (TNA T166/40)

Stephen Bunker described him as a patriot, Land Rover driver, steady smoker, avid reader, member of the Special Forces Club, organiser of the Bedford branch of the Campaign for Nuclear Disarmament and Elder of the Bedford Presbyterian Church. He worked for several years as a Labour Councillor for Putnoe ward before joining the Liberals in 1959, possibly over the nuclear weapons issue. Shortly after retiring as major when he reached the age of 60, he suffered a heart attack and died in 1961.

A week after his funeral a letter was published in the Bedfordshire Times in the name of a number of his friends. It noted that 'his passing is more than just a loss of an individual. To us he was embodiment of an ideal, always in his own way striving after the betterment of society. His vision was broad and embraced all mankind, and he spent himself on its behalf.

(Bunker, S. op.cit.p.14)

Bibliography

Bunker, S. (2007), *The Spy Capital of Britain : Bedfordshire's secret war 1939-1945,* Bedford Chronicles

Crawley, A. 'The Limpet Mine & 171-175 Tavistock Street', *BAALHS,* (April 2012)

Foot, M.R.D. (1999), The Special Operations Executive 1940 - 1946, Pimlico, London

Macrae, S. (1971), *Winston Churchill's Toyshop,* Kineton, The Roundwood Press

Sweet-Escott, B. (1965), *Baker Street Irregular.* Methuen, London,

McDonnell, P.K. (2004), *Operatives, Spies and Saboteurs,* Citadel Press,

Turner, D. (2006), *Station XII Aston House SOE's Secret Centre,* Sutton

Wildman, R. and Crawley, A. (2003), *Bedford's Motoring Heritage,* Sutton Publishing

Websites

http://www.bbc.co.uk/ww2peopleswar/stories/97/a4372797.shtml

http://www.bbc.co.uk/ww2peopleswar/stories/52/a5961152.shtml

http://www.bbc.co.uk/ww2peopleswar/stories/34/a5961134.shtml

http://www.combinedops.com/Cockleshell%20Heroes.htm

http://www.realmilitaryflix.com/public/253.cfm

http://www.realmilitaryflix.com/public/203.cfm?sd=61

Bernard O'Connor's publications on SECRET operations during WW2

RAF Tempsford: Churchill's MOST SECRET Airfield, Amberley Publishing, (2010) 978-
The Women of RAF Tempsford: Heroines of Wartime Resistance**,** Amberley Publishing, (2011) 978-1445604343
Churchill and Stalin's Secret Agents: Operation Pickaxe at RAF Tempsford**,** Fonthill Media, (2011) 978-1781550021
The Tempsford Academy: Churchill and Roosevelt's Secret Airfield**,** Fonthill Media, (2012) 978-1781550038
Agent Rose: The True Story of Eileen Nearne, Britain's Forgotten Wartime Heroine, Amberley Publishing, (2010) 978-1445608389
Churchill's Angels: How Britain's Women Secret Agents Changed the Course of the Second World War**,** Amberley Publishing, (2012) 978-1445608280
The Courier: Reminiscences of a Female Secret Agent in Wartime France**,** (2010) www.lulu.com 978-1-902810-51-5
Designer: The True Story of Jacqueline Nearne, (2011) www.lulu.com, 978-1-291-06595-4
The Bedford Spy School, (2012) www.lulu.com, 978-1-291-06595-4
Bedford School's Secret Old Boys**,**(2012) www.lulu.com, 9781291300581
Return to Belgium, (2011) www.lulu.com 978-1-291-06595-4
Return to Holland, (2011) www.lulu.com, 978-1-291-06595-4
Nobby Clarke: Churchill's Backroom Boy, (2011) www.lulu.com, 978-1-291-06595-4
Charles Bovill: Radio Communication Expert during World War Two, (2011) www.lulu.com, 978-1-291-06595-4
Frank Nelson: The First Head of the Special Operations Executive, (2011) www.lulu.com, 978-1-291-06595-4
The Coffee Party: Soviet Agents destined for Austria in

World War Two, (2011) ***(Historical faction)*** www.lulu.com
Henri Dericourt: Triple agent? (2013) www.lulu.com
Sabotage in Denmark, (2013) www.lulu.com
Sabotage in Norway, (2013) www.lulu.com
Sabotage in Belgium, (2013) www.lulu.com
Sabotage in Belgium, (2013) www.lulu.com
Churchill's School for Saboteurs, Amberley Publishing ***(2013)***
Sabotage in France, (2013) www.lulu.com
Blackmail Sabotage, (2013) www.lulu.com

For details of these and his other publications on Bedfordshire visit his author spotlight:

http://www.lulu.com/spotlight/coprolite

Find out more about Bernard O'Connor's research by visiting: -
www.bernardoconnor.org.uk

www.ingramcontent.com/pod-product-compliance
Ingram Content Group UK Ltd.
Pitfield, Milton Keynes, MK11 3LW, UK
UKHW020234250726
13967UKWH00001B/354